The Texas Longhorns®

BY
MARK STEWART

NORWOODHOUSE PRESS
CHICAGO, ILLINOIS

Norwood House Press
P.O. Box 316598
Chicago, Illinois 60631

For information regarding Norwood House Press, please visit our website at:
www.norwoodhousepress.com or call 866-565-2900.

All photos courtesy of Icon SMI except the following:
The Associated Press (6, 8, 17, 22, 25, 33 & 36 right); Fiction House, Inc. (7);
Sports Review Publishing Co. (14); SA•GE Collectibles, Inc. (15, 37 top right, 40 bottom left & 41 top);
Time Inc./Sports Illustrated (16 & 30); Los Angeles Rams (24);
Author's Collection (31, 36 left & 41 bottom); True/Fawcett Publications (39);
Press Pass Inc. (37 top left & 40 top left); Matt Richman (48).
Cover Photo: Elsa/Getty Images

Editor: Mike Kennedy
Designer: Ron Jaffe
Project Management: Black Book Partners, LLC.
Editorial Production: Jessica McCulloch
Research: Joshua Zaffos

LIBRARY OF CONGRESS CATALOGING-IN-PUBLICATION DATA

Stewart, Mark, 1960-
  The Texas Longhorns / by Mark Stewart.
    p. cm. -- (Team spirit--college football)
  Includes bibliographical references and index.
  Summary: "Presents the history and accomplishments of The University of
Texas Longhorns football team. Includes highlights of players, coaches and
awards, longstanding rivalries, quotes, timelines, maps, glossary and
websites"--Provided by publisher.
  ISBN-13: 978-1-59953-280-6 (library edition : alk. paper)
  ISBN-10: 1-59953-280-8 (library edition : alk. paper) 1. Texas Longhorns
(Football team)--History--Juvenile literature. 2. University of Texas at
Austin--Football--History--Juvenile literature. I. Title.
  GV958.T45S74 2009
  796.332'630976431--dc22

                                          2008037482

Manufactured in the United States of America in North Mankato, Minnesota.
N144-012010

COVER PHOTO: The Longhorns celebrate a game-winning touchdown
during the 2004 season.

Table of Contents

SPORTS WORDS & VOCABULARY WORDS: In this book, you will find many words that are new to you. You also may see familiar words used in new ways. The glossary on page 46 gives the meanings of football words, as well as "everyday" words that have special football meanings. These words appear in **bold type** throughout the book. The glossary on page 47 gives the meanings of vocabulary words that are not related to football. They appear in ***bold italic type*** throughout the book.

Meet the Longhorns

Football players are supposed to be big, fast, and tough. Fans of The University of Texas Longhorns like to think their players are a little bigger, a little faster, and a little tougher than everyone else's. For more than a *century*, the school has **recruited** the top players from Texas, where football is easily the state's most popular sport.

The Longhorns play in the Big 12 Conference. It includes schools from seven states stretching from Iowa to Texas. The teams are very *competitive*, and the fans take their football very seriously. Texas prides itself in putting a great team on the field year after year.

This book tells the story of the Longhorns football team. Everyone who wears the burnt orange and white uniform is part of a long and proud *tradition*. The players work together during games and help one another in the classroom. And years after their football days are done, they still belong to one big, happy family.

Limas Sweed and Jamaal Charles celebrate a touchdown during a 70–3 blowout of the University of Colorado in 2005.

Way Back When

ootball first arrived at The University of Texas *campus* in Austin in the early 1890s. The game made its way west thanks to students who had played football in the east, where the sport was very popular. In 1893, Jim Morrison and Paul and Ray McLane organized the first team at Texas. Soon the school was playing a full schedule against other colleges in the region. In 1895, the Longhorns went *undefeated* and did not allow a point.

The Longhorns' first star was Clyde Littlefield. He was a good **all-around** athlete with a strong arm. He also coached the team in the 1920s and 1930s. In 1934, Texas made headlines by beating the University of Notre Dame, 7–6. The Longhorns took their final step into the national spotlight when they hired Dana X. Bible as their football coach in 1937.

Bible made Austin the place where every Texas high school star wanted to play. During the 1941 season, the Longhorns reached the top spot in the national rankings for the first time. They were even featured on the cover of *Life* magazine.

In 1944, Bobby Layne joined the Longhorns. He was bright, tough, and talented. Layne was a terrific passer and powerful runner. He never seemed to get tired or hurt. With Layne, Texas had a chance to win every time it took the field.

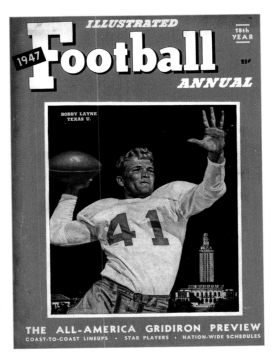

In 1957, Darrell Royal became coach of the Longhorns. Under Royal, the team would enjoy its greatest success. In 1963, Texas was crowned national champion. Quarterback Duke Carlisle and defensive lineman Scott Appleton led the Longhorns to many thrilling victories that year. Another member of the team was linebacker Tommy Nobis. He was the Longhorns' biggest star during the 1960s.

In 1969, Texas reached the top of the college football world again. The Longhorns had begun using a **wishbone formation**, which placed three runners behind the quarterback. The team won thanks to the strong arm and quick feet of quarterback James Street and the running of Ted Koy and Steve Worster. Koy's father, Ernie, had starred for the Longhorns in the 1930s. Texas had another great season in 1970.

LEFT: Dana X. Bible watches the action from the sideline in 1946.
ABOVE: Bobby Layne was front page news in 1947.

7

The Longhorns shared the national championship with The Ohio State University Buckeyes.

For many years, Texas was criticized for having no minority players on its roster. During the 1970s, the school recruited African-American student-athletes, the first of whom was Julius Whittier in 1976. The team's African-American leaders of the 1970s and 1980s included defensive stars Raymond Clayborn, Johnnie Johnson, and Kenneth Sims, receivers Johnny "Lam" Jones and Alfred Jackson, and runners Roosevelt Leaks and Earl Campbell. In 1977, Campbell won the **Heisman Trophy**. That year, Texas was ranked #1 until a loss to Notre Dame in the **Cotton Bowl**.

The Longhorns went through ups and downs in the 1980s and 1990s. Their top players included Kiki DeAyala, Jerry Gray, Tony Degrate, Eric Metcalf, and Ricky Williams. In 1998, Williams became the second Longhorn to win the Heisman Trophy.

In December of 1997, Texas hired Mack Brown to coach the team. Brown's goal was to build a championship program. With so many colleges competing for the state's best players, Brown's job was to convince the homegrown talent to stay in the Lone Star State and play for the Longhorns.

LEFT: Ricky Williams dodges a tackle. He was the second Texas player to win the Heisman Trophy. **ABOVE**: Earl Campbell takes a handoff. He set the stage for Williams during the 1970s.

21st Century

Under Mack Brown, Texas started building a powerful squad at the end of the 1990s. In 2004, the Longhorns went 11–1 and beat the University of Michigan in the **Rose Bowl**. The stars of that team included Derrick Johnson, Cedric Benson, Rod Wright, Michael Huff, Jonathan Scott, and Vince Young.

One year later, Texas went undefeated during the regular season. Young and the Longhorns were unstoppable. All that stood between them and the nation's top ranking was the University of Southern California (USC). The Longhorns beat the Trojans in the Rose Bowl to reach their goal.

With one national championship under their belts in the 21st century, the Longhorns and their fans are hungry for more. Every time the team takes the field, they are not only a part of history— they have a chance to make a little history of their own.

Tully Janszen congratulates Vince Young after a touchdown during a 2005 game.

Home Turf

The first football field used by the Longhorns was Clark Field. They played there starting in the 1890s. By the 1920s, the wooden stands at Clark Field could no longer hold the large crowds coming to see Texas games. In early November of the 1924 season, the Longhorns moved into Texas Memorial Stadium. For many years, it was known as the largest sports stadium of its kind in the Southwest.

The stadium has been ***modernized*** and enlarged several times in the years since. From 1969 to 1995, the playing surface was artificial turf. The Longhorns changed back to natural grass in 1996. That year, the field was renamed Darrell K Royal-Texas Memorial Stadium in honor of the team's beloved coach. In 2006, Texas installed the largest Daktronics video board in the nation in the stadium's south end.

BY THE NUMBERS

- *There are 94,113 seats in the Longhorns' stadium.*
- *The south end video board is 134 feet wide and 55 feet high.*
- *Texas played Baylor University in the stadium's first game on November 8, 1924.*

The Longhorns take the field at Darrell K Royal-Texas Memorial Stadium before a 2007 game.

Dressed for Success

The Texas football team was called the Steers during its early years. In 1903, *The Daily Texan* campus newspaper began calling them the Longhorns. Fans liked it, and the name stuck.

The team's helmet is white with an image of the head of a longhorn on each side. The Texas longhorn is a special breed of cattle that can survive in almost any environment. They can even eat cactus!

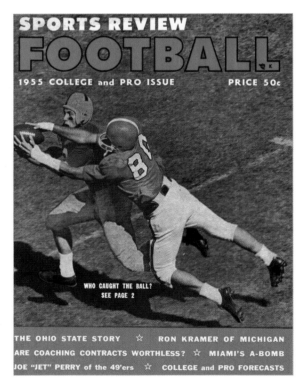

Orange has been a school color at Texas since the 1880s. But not until 1900 did the students vote to make orange and white the official colors. The players wore bright orange uniforms for many years, but the jerseys often faded to yellow by the end of the season. In 1928, the Longhorns switched to the darker burnt orange they use today.

This magazine cover from the 1950s shows a player in the Texas orange and white uniform.

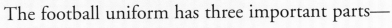

The football uniform has three important parts—
- Helmet
- Jersey
- Pants

Helmets used to be made out of leather, and they did not have facemasks—ouch! Today, helmets are made of super-strong plastic. The uniform top, or jersey, is made of thick fabric. It fits snugly around a player so that tacklers cannot grab it and pull him down. The pants come down just over the knees.

There is a lot more to a football uniform than what you see on the outside. Air can be pumped inside the helmet to give it a snug, padded fit. The jersey covers shoulder pads and sometimes a rib protector called a flak jacket. The pants include pads that protect the hips, thighs, *tailbone*, and knees.

Football teams have two sets of uniforms— one dark and one light. This makes it easier to tell the two teams apart on the field. Almost all teams wear their dark uniforms at home and their light ones on the road.

Jamaal Charles wears the 2007 Texas all-white road uniform.

25 *Jamaal* CHARLES RB

We're Number 1!

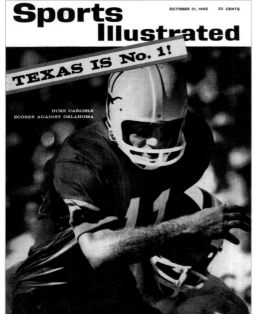

T he Longhorns have finished the year as national champions four times. In 1963, Texas began the season as one of the top teams in the country. The Longhorns defeated strong teams from the University of Oklahoma and the University of Arkansas to rise to #1.

The hero of the season was Duke Carlisle, the team's quarterback. Coach Darrell Royal also used Carlisle on defense. In a game against Baylor, the Longhorns held a 7–0 lead with 29 seconds left. Carlisle made a leaping **interception** to save the game. Against Texas A&M, he scored the winning touchdown with just over a minute left.

The Longhorns finished off their championship season by defeating the U.S. Naval Academy 28–6 in the Cotton Bowl. Tommy Nobis and Scott Appleton bottled up Navy's scrambling quarterback, Roger Staubach, all day long.

The Longhorns enjoyed championship seasons again in 1969 and 1970. No one could stop Royal's wishbone running attack. In 1969,

quarterback James Street led Texas to a thrilling 15–14 victory over Arkansas at the end of the year. The win assured Texas of the nation's top ranking. Street was the hero again in the Cotton Bowl. He led the Longhorns on a 76-yard touchdown drive in the fourth quarter to defeat Notre Dame 21–17.

Early in the 1970 season, UCLA found a way to stop the wishbone. However, the Bruins could not stop new Texas quarterback Eddie Phillips. With just a few seconds left in the game, Phillips threw a 45-yard touchdown pass to Cotton Speyrer for a 20–17 win. The

LEFT: Duke Carlisle and the #1 Longhorns were headline news in 1963.
ABOVE: Darrell Royal talks things over with Eddie Phillips in 1970.

Longhorns finished the year with a victory over Arkansas. It was the team's 30th win in a row. Notre Dame snapped the school's winning streak in the Cotton Bowl, but Texas was still good enough to share the national championship with Ohio State.

Texas returned to the top of college football in 2005. Michael Huff and Rod Wright led the defense, but it was the offense that powered the Longhorns all year long. Jonathan Scott *anchored* the offensive line. He and his teammates opened holes for the team's runners and protected passer Vince Young.

Young was a game-changing quarterback. He threw with great strength and accuracy and ran with tremendous speed and power. When Young was on his game, no defense could handle the Longhorns. They won every game they played, including the Big 12 Championship. In that game, Young led the Longhorns to a 70–3 win over the University of Colorado. Texas finished the year with 652 points—at the time the most in college history.

Young's finest moment came against USC in January. The Trojans entered the **Bowl Championship Series (BCS)** Championship game ranked #1. Texas was #2. USC had a pair of Heisman Trophy candidates in Reggie Bush and Matt Leinart. But Young was the brightest star of the night. He ran for 200 yards and passed for 267.

The Longhorns trailed by 12 points late in the fourth quarter when Young took over. He darted through the Trojans for a 17-yard

Vince Young crosses the goal line for the winning touchdown against USC in the 2006 Rose Bowl.

touchdown run to make the score 38–33. After the Texas defense held USC, Young spearheaded a 56-yard touchdown drive. He produced the winning score on a fourth-down run from the eight yard line with 19 seconds left. He added a **two-point conversion** to make the final score 41–38.

Go-To Guys

TOMMY NOBIS
Linebacker

- BORN: 9/20/1943
- PLAYED FOR VARSITY: 1963–1965

Tommy Nobis was speedy, strong, and smart. He could sack the quarterback, pull down a running back, or cover a pass receiver. Nobis won the Maxwell Award in 1965 as the nation's top player.

EARL CAMPBELL
Running Back

- BORN: 3/29/1955
- PLAYED FOR VARSITY: 1974–1977

Earl Campbell was like a runaway truck when he had the football. Tacklers bounced off of him when he went up the middle, and no one could catch him once he broke free. Campbell gained 4,444 yards in four years and became the first Longhorn to win the Heisman Trophy, in 1977.

KENNETH SIMS
Defensive Lineman

- BORN: 10/31/1959
- PLAYED FOR VARSITY: 1978–1981

Kenneth Sims and teammate Steve McMichael gave the Longhorns an awesome defensive line. Both players exploded into action the instant the ball was snapped. Sims won the Lombardi Award as the nation's top lineman in 1981.

RICKY WILLIAMS Running Back

- BORN: 5/21/1977   • PLAYED FOR VARSITY: 1995–1998

Ricky Williams keyed the Longhorns' powerful offense in the late 1990s. Williams was a swift and powerful runner who set a record with 6,279 career rushing yards. He was named the country's top running back twice and won the Heisman Trophy as a senior.

DERRICK JOHNSON   Linebacker

- BORN: 11/22/1982
- PLAYED FOR VARSITY: 2001–2004

Derrick Johnson made Texas fans remember the days of Tommy Nobis. "DJ" was a quick and powerful linebacker. In 2004, Johnson won the Butkus Award as the top college linebacker and the Nagurski Trophy as the nation's best defensive player.

VINCE YOUNG   Quarterback

- BORN: 5/18/1983
- PLAYED FOR VARSITY: 2003–2005

Vince Young became the Longhorns' starting quarterback as a sophomore. He won 20 games in a row, including the national championship contest against USC. Young was the **Most Valuable Player (MVP)** of the Rose Bowl twice and won the Maxwell Award in 2005.

Derrick Johnson

21

JACK CRAIN Running Back

- BORN: 1/7/1920 • DIED: 10/22/1994 • PLAYED FOR VARSITY: 1939–1941

Speedy Jack Crain was the finest player in the **Southwest Conference** in 1939 and 1940. He set an example of excellence that helped the Texas football team become one of the best in the country.

BOBBY LAYNE Quarterback

- BORN: 12/19/1926 • DIED: 12/1/1986
- PLAYED FOR VARSITY: 1944–1947

Bobby Layne came to Austin on a baseball scholarship, but coach Dana X. Bible talked him into trying out for the football team. Layne completed daring passes and made amazing runs. He was the first Longhorn whose brilliant talent caused fans to jump out of their seats.

CHRIS GILBERT Running Back

- BORN: 10/16/1946
- PLAYED FOR VARSITY: 1966–1968

Between the championship years of 1963 and 1969, the Longhorns' best runner was Chris Gilbert. He gained more than 1,000 yards in each of his three varsity seasons. Gilbert's 96-yard touchdown run in 1967 is still the longest in team history.

DUKE CARLISLE · Quarterback

- BORN: 12/13/1941 · PLAYED FOR VARSITY: 1961–1963

Whether passing or running, Duke Carlisle was one of those players who could always find a way to win. He led the Longhorns to their first national championship. Carlisle also was a valuable defensive player.

ROOSEVELT LEAKS · Running Back

- BORN: 1/31/1953
- PLAYED FOR VARSITY: 1972–1974

Roosevelt Leaks used his blinding speed to gain 342 yards in a 1973 game against Southern Methodist University. Later that year, he finished third in the voting for the Heisman Trophy. Along with tight end Julius Whittier, Leaks was one of the Longhorns' first African-American stars.

ROY WILLIAMS · Receiver

- BORN: 12/20/1981
- PLAYED FOR VARSITY: 2000–2003

No one ever figured out how to stop big, strong Roy Williams. He caught passes in 47 games in a row and broke almost every school record for receivers.

LEFT: Chris Gilbert
RIGHT: Roy Williams

BUD McFADIN   Offensive/Defensive Lineman

• BORN: 8/21/1928   • DIED: 2/13/2006   • PLAYED FOR VARSITY: 1948–1950

Bud McFadin played offensive guard and defensive tackle for the Longhorns. He was conference MVP as a senior. McFadin also was named MVP of the 1951 Cotton Bowl, his final college game.

JAMES SAXTON   Running Back

• BORN: 5/21/1940   • PLAYED FOR VARSITY: 1959–1961

James Saxton caught rabbits with his hands as a boy. When he played for Texas, he left tacklers clutching at thin air. Saxton and Jack Collins gave the Longhorns a great running game. Coach Darrell Royal once compared Saxton's running style to the movements a balloon makes once the air is let loose.

SCOTT APPLETON   Defensive Lineman

• BORN: 2/20/1942   • DIED: 3/2/1992   • PLAYED FOR VARSITY: 1961–1963

Scott Appleton used his speed and intelligence to stop runners in their tracks. In 1963, he captained Texas to the national championship. That year, Appleton became the first Longhorn to win the Outland Trophy as the nation's top lineman.

JAMES STREET Quarterback

- BORN: 4/9/1948 • PLAYED FOR VARSITY: 1968–1969

Only a handful of college quarterbacks can claim they never lost a game, and James Street is one of them. He was 20–0 as a starter. Street was the first player to master the wishbone offense created by Darrell Royal. Street also pitched the Texas baseball team to the **College World Series** three times. His son Huston was a star pitcher for the Longhorns, too.

TONY BRACKENS Defensive Lineman

- BORN: 12/26/1974
- PLAYED FOR VARSITY: 1993–1995

Tony Brackens grew up on his family's ranch and was used to working hard from dawn to dusk. Football was easy by comparison! Brackens never gave up on a play and made tackles all over the field. He was named **all-conference** three times.

MICHAEL HUFF Defensive Back

- BORN: 3/6/1983
- PLAYED FOR VARSITY: 2002–2005

Michael Huff won the Jim Thorpe Award as the nation's best defensive back in 2005. In the BCS Championship against USC, he made several key plays—including the tackle that got Texas the ball back for its game-winning touchdown drive.

LEFT: Bud McFadin
RIGHT: Tony Brackens

25

On the Sidelines

The Texas football team spent 40 years searching for the perfect coach. The school finally found him in 1937. Dana X. Bible had one of the best football minds in the country. Under Bible, the Longhorns became the best team in the region. In Bible's final five years, the Longhorns were conference champions three times.

Bible retired in 1946, but stayed on to run the school's athletics program. In 1957, he hired Darrell Royal, who coached Texas for 20 seasons. During those years, the Longhorns finished among the country's Top 5 teams nine times—and won three national championships.

In December of 1997, Mack Brown arrived in Austin. He asked his players for two things—excellence and consistency. They responded by winning 10 games or more year after year. In the 2005 season, Brown watched with pride as the Longhorns surprised the football world and beat USC in the Rose Bowl. The victory sealed the school's fourth national title.

Mack Brown holds up a trophy celebrating the Longhorns' 2005 championship season.

Rivals

Many schools consider Texas to be their greatest *rival*. If you ask Texas fans about their toughest rivals, they will give two answers: Texas A&M and Oklahoma.

Texas and Texas A&M battle for state bragging rights every year. The Longhorns and the Aggies have faced each other more than 100 times. Their game is called the State Farm Lone Star Showdown. The contest is usually played on Thanksgiving Day.

The Texas–Oklahoma rivalry also dates back more than 100 years. In fact, when the two teams first played in 1900, Oklahoma wasn't even a state yet! Part of the border between Texas and Oklahoma is formed by the Red River. That is why the game between the two teams is called the AT&T Red River Rivalry. The contest is played in the Cotton Bowl in Dallas, which is located in between the schools.

Some of the most exciting games in Texas history have come against Oklahoma. In 1958, Bob Bryant caught the winning touchdown pass in a 15–14 victory by the Longhorns. It was Darrell Royal's second Red River Rivalry game as the coach of Texas. A *decade* earlier, he had played quarterback for Oklahoma! In 1977, two Texas quarterbacks were injured early in the game

Peter Gardere drops back to pass. He became a hero in Texas after beating Oklahoma four years in a row.

against the Sooners. Earl Campbell rescued Texas and stampeded over Oklahoma. The Longhorns won 13–6.

How big is this rivalry? From 1989 to 1992, Peter Gardere became the first Texas quarterback to win the Oklahoma game four years in a row. Fans will never forget him. He is still known on campus as "Peter the Great."

One Great Day

The 1969 season marked the 100th anniversary of college football in America. To finish the year in style, Texas and Arkansas agreed to make their meeting the last game of the season. By kickoff time,

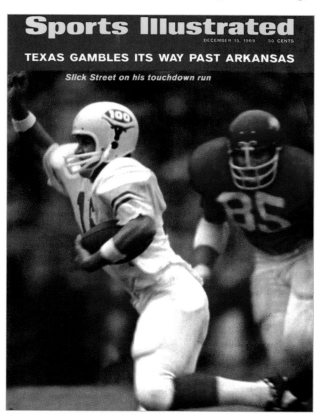

the Longhorns had risen to the top of the national rankings. The Razorbacks were close behind at #2. President Richard Nixon flew to Arkansas to watch the game and honor the winner of the national championship. Many fans were calling this the "Game of the Century."

As expected, the contest was a tough battle. Arkansas led 14–0 after three quarters. Quarterback James Street sparked a Texas comeback when he scrambled for a touchdown and then made a two-point conversion. The score

was now 14–8. Moments later, the Longhorns stopped a long drive by the Razorbacks with an interception in the end zone.

With less than five minutes to play, Texas faced a crucial fourth down. The Razorbacks prepared for a running play, but the Longhorns fooled them with a pass. Street dropped back and looked for tight end Randy Peschel. When the Arkansas defense froze, Street lofted a long bomb. Peschel ran under the ball and brought it in for a big gain. The play shocked Arkansas. Texas scored minutes later and went ahead 15–14. The Longhorns intercepted another pass to complete their victory and win the national championship.

LEFT: *Sports Illustrated* called James Street "Slick" in its story about the 1969 Texas–Arkansas game.   **ABOVE**: Texas fans were proud to wave pennants like this one after the Longhorns' national championship.

It Really Happened

Texas fans may argue about the best quarterback or running back in school history, but they all agree on the Longhorns' greatest kicker. Russell Erxleben's leg was so powerful that no kick seemed too far for him. His kickoffs flew out of the end zone. His punts sailed over the heads of opponents. And he kicked 50-yard field goals like he was practicing in his backyard.

In the 1970s, more and more teams used **soccer-style** kickers. Erxleben was "old school"—he kicked the ball straight-on. In a 1977 game against Rice University, the Longhorns faced fourth down at midfield. Coach Fred Akers waved the field goal team onto the field. A buzz went through the crowd as Erxleben stood near his own 40 yard line.

The ball was snapped and placed at the 43 yard line. Erxleben took two steps and crushed the ball with his right foot. It soared into the air, through the end zone, and between the goal posts for three points—67 yards in all.

"I'll never forget the sound it made when he hit it," said Akers. "It was like a gunshot."

Russell Erxleben boots a field goal with his straight-on kicking style.

No one had ever made a kick from that distance. The most amazing thing is that Erxleben's kick kept going more than 10 yards past the goal posts. Akers believes it would have been good from 75 yards!

Team Spirit

The Longhorns have been playing football for more than 100 years. The players and fans have many great traditions. The most popular is the "Hook 'em, Horns" sign. The thumb and pinky are held out while the middle fingers are closed tight. This looks like a longhorn's head. Students and players also love to sing the school's fight song, "The Eyes of Texas." It is sung to the same tune as "I've Been Working on the Railroad."

The people of Austin always know when the Longhorns have won a game, because the university's famous tower is lit up in orange, or orange and white. This tradition began in the 1930s. The tower also is lit for important academic achievements.

Another great football tradition is the team's *mascot*, a Texas longhorn named Bevo. The first Bevo arrived in 1916. Unfortunately, the team ate him at a banquet in 1920. In the years since, each Bevo has been treated more kindly.

Bevo is led onto the field after a victory by Texas in 2005.

Timeline

At the end of each college season, the best teams are invited to play in special "Bowl" games, such as the Rose Bowl, **Orange Bowl**, and **Sugar Bowl**. Bowl games usually take place in January, but they count in the final rankings of the previous season. That means the top team in 2007 wasn't decided until early 2008. In this timeline, bowl games are listed in the year they were held.

1893
The team wins its first game 18–16 against a club team from Dallas.

1916
The Longhorns are Southwest Conference champions for the first time.

1945
Hub Bechtol is the team's first *consensus* **All-American**.

1957
Darrell Royal is hired as head coach.

Texas fans have been wearing pins like this one for nearly 100 years.

Hub Bechtol

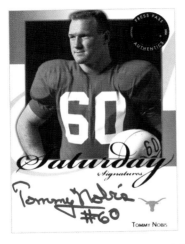

Tommy Nobis, a star for the 1963 champs.

Vince Young

1963
The Longhorns are national champs.

1998
Ricky Williams wins the Heisman Trophy.

2006
Vince Young leads the Longhorns to victory in the Rose Bowl.

1970
The Longhorns win their third national title.

1977
Earl Campbell wins the Heisman Trophy.

2001
Major Applewhite sets a school record with 473 passing yards in a game.

Major Applewhite looks for a receiver.

Fun Facts

PLAN B

In the first game played on the Texas campus, the football popped when a group of players piled up after a tackle. The game was delayed until someone could bicycle to a store and buy a replacement.

NO OX-IDENT

In the early 1930s, Texas had two large and powerful linemen with the same nickname. "Ox" Emerson and "Ox" Blanton made the Longhorns one of the best teams in the nation.

400 CLUB

As of 2008, only three Texas quarterbacks have had 400 total yards (passing and running) in a game. Vince Young did it three times, and Chris Simms and Major Applewhite each did it once.

LEFT: Chris Simms
RIGHT: Bobby Layne

RUNNING & JUMPING

Eric Metcalf was an all-conference running back three years in a row during the 1980s. He also was *National Collegiate Athletic Association (NCAA)* long jump champion twice.

ONE-MAN GANG

In the 1946 Cotton Bowl, Bobby Layne ran for three touchdowns, caught one, threw for two more,

and kicked four **extra points**. He was responsible for every point in a 40–27 victory over the University of Missouri.

KEEPING UP WITH THE JONESES

In 1977, the Longhorns had three players named Johnny Jones. To tell them apart, the team used three nicknames for the trio—Lam, Ham, and Jam. In the 1978 **Sun Bowl**, the Joneses gained a total of 211 yards, as Texas beat the University of Maryland 42–0.

For the Record

The great Longhorns teams and players have left their marks on the record books. These are the "best of the best" …

LONGHORNS AWARD WINNERS

HEISMAN TROPHY
TOP COLLEGE PLAYER

Earl Campbell	1977
Ricky Williams	1998

MAXWELL AWARD
TOP COLLEGE PLAYER

Tommy Nobis	1965
Ricky Williams	1998
Vince Young	2005

WALTER CAMP AWARD
TOP COLLEGE PLAYER

Ricky Williams	1998

DAVEY O'BRIEN AWARD
TOP QUARTERBACK

Vince Young	2005

DOAK WALKER AWARD
TOP RUNNING BACK

Ricky Williams	1997
Ricky Williams	1998
Cedric Benson	2004

JIM THORPE AWARD
TOP DEFENSIVE BACK

Michael Huff	2005
Aaron Ross	2006

OUTLAND TROPHY
TOP LINEMAN

Scott Appleton	1963
Tommy Nobis	1965
Brad Shearer	1977

VINCE LOMBARDI AWARD
TOP LINEMAN

Kenneth Sims	1981
Tony Degrate	1984

BRONKO NAGURSKI AWARD
TOP DEFENSIVE PLAYER

Derrick Johnson	2004

DICK BUTKUS AWARD
TOP LINEBACKER

Derrick Johnson	2004

Michael Huff

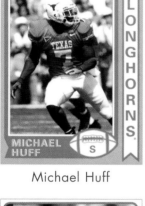

Aaron Ross

Cedric Benson

LONGHORNS ACHIEVEMENTS

ACHIEVEMENT	YEAR
Southwest Conference Champions	1916
Southwest Conference Champions	1918
Southwest Conference Champions	1920
Southwest Conference Champions	1928
Southwest Conference Champions	1930
Southwest Conference Champions	1942
Southwest Conference Champions	1943
Southwest Conference Champions	1945
Southwest Conference Champions	1950
Southwest Conference Champions	1952
Southwest Conference Champions*	1953
Southwest Conference Champions*	1959
Southwest Conference Champions*	1961
Southwest Conference Champions	1962
Southwest Conference Champions	1963
National Champions	1963
Southwest Conference Champions*	1968
Southwest Conference Champions	1969
National Champions	1969
Southwest Conference Champions	1970
National Champions	1970
Southwest Conference Champions	1971
Southwest Conference Champions	1972
Southwest Conference Champions	1973
Southwest Conference Champions*	1975
Southwest Conference Champions	1977
Southwest Conference Champions	1983
Southwest Conference Champions	1990
Southwest Conference Champions*	1994
Southwest Conference Champions	1995
Big 12 South Champions	1996
Big 12 Champions	1996
Big 12 South Champions	1999
Big 12 South Champions	2001
Big 12 South Champions	2005
Big 12 Champions	2005
National Champions	2005

Shared this honor with another school.

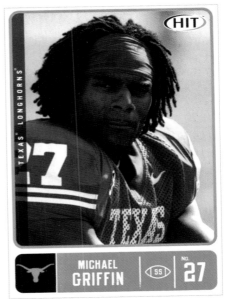

Michael Griffin, who starred with Michael Huff and Aaron Ross for the 2005 national champs.

The Longhorns have enjoyed many great victories, including their win in the 1948 Sugar Bowl.

The Big 12 Conference

From 1914 to 1995, the Longhorns were members of the Southwest Conference. In 1996, four teams from this conference joined with the teams from the Big Eight Conference. They formed a new conference called the Big 12 Conference. The Big 12 has a North Division and South Division in football.

THE BIG 12 CONFERENCE

FOOTBALL NORTH DIVISION

1   Iowa State University Cyclones
    Ames, Iowa

2   Kansas State University Wildcats
    Manhattan, Kansas

3   University of Colorado Buffaloes
    Boulder, Colorado

4   University of Kansas Jayhawks
    Lawrence, Kansas

5   University of Missouri Tigers
    Columbia, Missouri

6   University of Nebraska Cornhuskers
    Lincoln, Nebraska

FOOTBALL SOUTH DIVISION

7   Baylor University Bears
    Waco, Texas

8   Oklahoma State University Cowboys
    Stillwater, Oklahoma

9   Texas A&M Aggies
    College Station, Texas

10   Texas Tech University Red Raiders
    Lubbock, Texas

11   University of Oklahoma Sooners
    Norman, Oklahoma

12   The University of Texas Longhorns
    Austin, Texas

The College Game

College football may look like the same game you see NFL teams play on Sundays, but there are some important differences. The first is that most college games take place on Saturday. This has been true for more than 100 years. Below are several other differences between college and pro football.

CLASS NOTES

College players are younger than NFL players. They are full-time student-athletes, having graduated from high school and having been recruited to play on their college's varsity team. Most are between the ages of 17 and 23.

College players are allowed to compete for four seasons. Each year is given a different name or "class"—freshman (first year), sophomore (second year), junior (third year), and senior (fourth year). Players who are unable to play for the varsity can remain in the same class for an extra year. This is called "red-shirting." These players are still students and must attend classes during their extra year.

RULE BOOK

There are several differences between the rules in college football and the NFL. Here are the important ones: 1) In college, a play ends as soon as the ball carrier's knee touches the ground, even if he slips or dives. In the NFL, a player must be tackled. 2) In college, a player catching the ball near the sideline must have one foot in bounds for the reception to count. In the NFL, a player must have both feet in bounds. 3) Since 1996, tie games in college have been decided by a special overtime period. Each team is given a chance to score from its opponent's 25-yard line. In the NFL, the first team to score in overtime is the winner.

WHO'S NUMBER 1?

How is the national champion of college football decided? Each week during the season, teams are ranked from best to worst in several different polls of coaches and sportswriters. These rankings are based on many factors, including a team's record and the level of competition that it has played. At the end of the year, the two top-ranked teams play each other. The winner is declared the national champion. This tradition started in 1998 when college football began using the BCS. Prior to that year, the top two teams did not always face each other. Sometimes, that made it very difficult to decide which school was the best.

CONFERENCE CALL

Most colleges are members of athletic conferences. Each conference represents a different part of the country. For example, the Atlantic Coast Conference is made up of teams from up and down the East Coast. Teams that belong to a conference are required to play a certain number of games against the other teams in their conference. At the end of the year, the team with the best record is crowned conference champion (unless the league holds a championship game). Teams also play schools from outside their conference. Wins and losses in those games do not count in the conference standings. However, they are very important to a team's national ranking.

BOWL GAMES

Bowl games—such as the Rose Bowl, Fiesta Bowl, Sugar Bowl, and Orange Bowl—are extra games played at the end of each season. Bowl games give fans a chance to see the best teams from around the country play one another. These games are scheduled during the Christmas and New Year's holiday season, so students and fans are free to travel to the cities where bowl games are played. There are now more than 25 bowl games.

Since 1998, the BCS has selected the nation's very best teams and carefully matched them in a handful of bowl games. The BCS chooses the champions of major conferences, as well as other schools with talented teams. The two top-ranked teams meet in the BCS title game for the national championship.

Glossary

FOOTBALL WORDS TO KNOW

ALL-AMERICAN—A college player voted as the best at his position.

ALL-AROUND—Good at many different parts of the game.

ALL-CONFERENCE—A college player voted as the best at his position in his conference.

BOWL CHAMPIONSHIP SERIES (BCS)—The system used by college football to select the best two teams to play for the national championship each season. Before the BCS came along, the national championship was unofficial, and more than one team often claimed they were the best.

COLLEGE WORLD SERIES—The championship series for college baseball teams.

COTTON BOWL—The annual bowl game played in Dallas, Texas. The first Cotton Bowl was played in 1937.

EXTRA POINTS—Kicks worth one point attempted after touchdowns.

HEISMAN TROPHY—The award given each year to the best player in college football.

INTERCEPTION—A pass that is caught by the defensive team.

MOST VALUABLE PLAYER (MVP)—The award given to the top player in each bowl game and an honor given each year by some conferences.

ORANGE BOWL—The annual bowl game played in Miami, Florida. The first Orange Bowl was played in 1935.

RECRUITED—Competed for a student-athlete. Each year colleges recruit the best high school players and offer them athletics scholarships.

ROSE BOWL—The annual bowl game played in Pasadena, California. The Tournament of Roses Parade takes place before the game. The first Rose Bowl was played in 1902.

SOCCER-STYLE—Approaching the ball on an angle, instead of straight on.

SOUTHWEST CONFERENCE—The conference that came before the Big 12 Conference.

SUGAR BOWL—The annual bowl game played in New Orleans, Louisiana. The first Sugar Bowl was played in 1935.

SUN BOWL—The annual bowl game played in El Paso, Texas. The first Sun Bowl was played in 1935.

TWO-POINT CONVERSION—A play following a touchdown where the offense tries to cross the goal line with the ball from the 2 yard line, instead of kicking an extra point.

WISHBONE FORMATION—A formation in which three running backs line up behind the quarterback in a triangle set that resembles a wishbone.

OTHER WORDS TO KNOW

ANCHORED—Held steady.

CAMPUS—The grounds and buildings of a college.

CENTURY—A period of 100 years.

COMPETITIVE—Having a strong desire to win.

CONSENSUS—Agreed upon by a large majority of voters.

DECADE—A period of 10 years; also specific periods, such as the 1950s.

MASCOT—An animal or person believed to bring a group good luck.

MODERNIZED—Brought up to date.

NATIONAL COLLEGIATE ATHLETIC ASSOCIATION (NCAA)—The largest governing body of college sports.

RIVAL—Extremely emotional competitor.

TAILBONE—The bone that protects the base of the spine.

TRADITION—A belief or custom that is handed down from generation to generation.

UNDEFEATED—Without a loss.

Places to Go

ON THE ROAD

THE UNIVERSITY OF TEXAS
1701 Red River Street
Austin, Texas 78768
(512) 471-4602

COLLEGE FOOTBALL HALL OF FAME
111 South St. Joseph Street
South Bend, Indiana 46601
(800) 440-3263

ON THE WEB

THE UNIVERSITY OF TEXAS LONGHORNS
  • *Learn more about the Longhorns*

www.texassports.com
www.mackbrown-texasfootball.com

BIG 12 CONFERENCE
  • *Learn more about the Big 12 Conference teams*

www.big12sports.com

COLLEGE FOOTBALL HALL OF FAME
  • *Learn more about college football*

www.collegefootball.org

ON THE BOOKSHELF

To learn more about the sport of football, look for these books at your library or bookstore:

  • DeCock, Luke. *Great Teams in College Football History*. Chicago, Illinois: Raintree, 2006.

  • Kaufman, Gabriel. *Football in the Big Ten*. New York, New York: Rosen Central, 2008.

  • Yuen, Kevin. *The 10 Most Intense College Football Rivalries*. New York, New York: Franklin Watts, 2008.

Index

PAGE NUMBERS IN **BOLD** REFER TO ILLUSTRATIONS.

About the Author

MARK STEWART has written more than 30 books on football players and teams, and over 100 sports books for kids. He also has interviewed dozens of athletes, politicians, and celebrities. Although Mark grew up in New York City, he became a Longhorns fan after a life-changing visit to Austin in 1982. He now has family in the Lone Star State and roots for Texas each season. Mark comes from a family of writers. His grandfather was Sunday Editor of *The New York Time*s and his mother was Articles Editor for *Ladies' Home Journal* and *McCall's*. Mark became interested in sports during lazy summer days spent at the Connecticut home of his father's godfather, sportswriter John R. Tunis. Mark is a graduate of Duke University, with a degree in History. He lives with his wife Sarah, and daughters Mariah and Rachel, overlooking Sandy Hook, New Jersey.